The Dallas Arboretum and Botanical Garden

"Let Nature Nurture You"

History of the Arboretum

In the 1960s in Dallas, members of the North Dallas Garden Forum were concerned that Dallas did not have a public botanic garden for its citizens, as did every other city of our size and larger in the nation. Many members had seen botanic gardens in other cities and knew what it did for the quality of life, the enjoyment of its citizens, the appreciation of horticulture, and what it could do for the environment of our area.

They joined forces with the Beautification Committee of the North Dallas Chamber of Commerce and together made appeals to the City of Dallas Park and Recreation Board for such a facility. The city had no land for such a garden, but it was open-minded to reconsidering the endeavor in the future, if it were financially feasible.

In 1977, the City of Dallas purchased the forty-four-acre DeGolyer estate from Southern Methodist University, which had received it from Everett DeGolyer Jr. Volunteers of the newly formed Dallas Arboretum and Botanical Society, Inc., made an appeal once again to the Park Board, and after proving they could financially manage the operation, began contractual talks with the city.

While these negotiations were taking place, the twenty-two-acre estate of Roberta and Alex Camp, adjacent to the DeGolyer property, was purchased by

Ralph Rogers, the Eugene McDermott Foundation, and others for the Botanical Society.

A contract was signed with the city and stated that the Dallas Arboretum and Botanical Society, Inc., would manage this land and the activities on it for the City of Dallas with terms that were advantageous to both parties. In turn, the Botanical Society turned over the ownership of the Camp Estate to the city, forming what is now the sixty-six acres of the Dallas Arboretum.

The selection of this site for the city's botanical garden seemed inspired. The DeGolyers cared very deeply about the grand trees on the property and the vistas it offered. The design of their home was such that it protected old trees and offered views of either the lake, the garden or the courtyards from every room.

They had engaged Arthur and Marie Berger, acclaimed landscape designers from California, to provide the original plan for their garden. In 1936 it was ahead of its time in this section of the country: an allee of magnolias, an allee of crape myrtles, a grove of pecan trees, a small area for Mrs. DeGolyer's own garden, a vegetable garden, and an orchard—leaving intact a vast woodland area—all of which enhanced the acreage that was once a dairy farm. In designing the house, a cutting room and greenhouse were also added and two gardeners were employed.

Roberta Camp also loved the view of the lake, but she preferred the enclosed feeling provided by having her estate surrounded by bamboo. Her home, designed by John Staub of Houston, offered three views of her acreage from each room, and this airy design brought the outside in.

The botanic garden has had three master plans for its development. The first was developed by Jones and Jones of Seattle. It was later refined to make it more acceptable to all the constituent groups of the Arboretum by Myrick and Santana. In 2001, an updated master plan was created by Andropogon Associates of Philadelphia. This was a comprehensive study of the needs of all the gardens' stakeholders and user groups, and from this and other land-use studies they gave the society's board the plan for the next twenty-five years.

The Dallas Arboretum and Botanical Society, Inc., has a board of sixty, a staff of over one hundred (with approximately a third of these in the horticultural area), and over six hundred volunteers giving more than forty-three thousand hours a year.

The Dallas Arboretum acknowledges the significant support from Mrs. Margaret McDermott, the Eugene McDermott Foundation, Mrs. Virginia Nick, Mrs. Nell Denman, Mr. Ralph Pinkus, Mr. Ralph Rogers, Mrs. Orien Woolf, Mr. Jim Coker, Brigadier General Bryghte Godbold, the Meadows Foundation, the Dallas Foundation, the Communities Foundation of Texas, the Hoblitzelle Foundation, the Hillcrest Foundation, every past chairman to date, and so many others for whom we will remain eternally grateful.

The Arboretum Today

Along the banks of Dallas' White Rock Lake, two families—Nell and Everette DeGolyer (known as "Mr. De") and Roberta and Alex Camp—built distinct homes that took advantage of the setting's natural beauty. Now, almost three quarters of a century later, their estates have developed into one of the most beloved gardens in the country and one of the most popular attractions in the city of Dallas— the Dallas Arboretum and Botanical Garden.

The Arboretum's mission has several aspects that have guided us these many years. We wish to represent the highest standards in horticultural excellence in our displays, offer educational programs to adults and children, provide research to the industry, and improve the horticultural offerings available, thereby enhancing our local landscapes.

Throughout the year, we change our displays and hold festivals for the community to enjoy. To enhance our themed presentations, we have added garden topiary design and floral buildings that have been duplicated around the country. Photographed so very often for magazines across the nation, the garden's appeal is noteworthy.

Our adult education programs now offer one hundred and twenty courses in the fall and spring on a wide variety of topics, which are taught by experts in the field. Our childhood education program sees close to eighty thousand school children a year in classes led by degreed teachers. We are known for showing teachers the best way to teach the science principles in kindergarten through sixth grade, with evaluations showing remarkable advances in retained learning from those who come to the best laboratory of all, the gardens of the Arboretum.

Our award-winning trial gardens provide the grounds for essential research that we offer back to our industry, showing the latest results from testing in the Texas heat and drought conditions. The results are selections that are offered at many national nurseries and have greatly improved the look of landscapes throughout the country, in addition to enhancing the displays of our own gardens.

We manage all of this in a financially responsible way, with our planning and results overseen by a sixty-member board of directors. The success of the arboretum is due to the dreams of our founders, the leadership of our board members, the diligence of a very capable staff, and the support of our many volunteers, all of whom work together to share this urban oasis with those who visit.

Each year, more than five hundred thousand visitors from over forty-six countries come to the garden, and they experience many of the vistas represented in this compendium. We are delighted to share them with you at this time and look forward to seeing you in the garden.

Cissy Thomsen Welcoming Water Wall

The Cissy Thomsen Welcoming Water Wall greets guests as they come to the main entry. The fountain design by Lake|Flato against the retaining wall is enhanced throughout the year with container displays. It was given by C.J. Thomsen, in the name of his wife, Cissy.

Trammell Crow Pavilion

The Trammell Crow Visitor Education Pavilion, named after the well-known Dallas businessman and philanthropist, was designed by Ted Flato of the Lake|Flato Architectural firm in San Antonio, Texas. The entire pavilion, opened in 2003, was funded by private donors and a bond issue from the City of Dallas. The interior of the Crow Pavilion is approximately forty thousand square feet, and its design embodies a village of structures made of Texas Lueders Limestone, walls of glass, and covered pathways and porches. With this design, the architects have allowed the gardens to be more important than the buildings.

Landscape architect Naud Burnett designed the transition area from the arboretum entrance into the Palmer Fern Dell and the Jonsson Color Garden.

The Wyatt-Wold Education Wing features two one-thousand-square-foot indoor classrooms, providing venues for expanded school field trip programs and year-round adult education classes. An outdoor area serves as a garden laboratory. Additional spaces include the Hillcrest Classroom, Green Classroom, Sewell Board Room, and the Meadows Orientation Theater, which features a high-definition film highlighting the arboretum and its programs.

The Scott Ginsburg Family Entrance Plaza is the main gathering place for those coming to the garden and meeting friends. From its entry, you can see the Lennox Information Booth, which leads to Rosine Hall, a five-thousand-square-foot venue given by the Rosine Fund of the Communities Foundation of Texas, as designated by the daughter of Rosine Sammons, Mary Ann Cree. It provides space for large meetings, lectures, meals, and receptions.

You can also see the Gisela H. Rodriguez Gazebo, a site for small gatherings and weddings, the Lula Mae Slaughter Outdoor Dining Terrace, which serves snacks and lunch daily, the Hoffman Family Gift Shop, and lastly the beautiful Jerry Junkins Fountain and Courtyard. The tree in the center of the plaza is dedicated to Anthony Grant Glover and Luke Anthony Glover by Trudy and Bob Ladd.

Bella Via

The Bella Via, "Beautiful Walkway," was given in honor of Morgan Ann Ladd and Katherine Elise Ladd, the granddaughters of Trudy and Bob Ladd. It provides the link between the Scott Ginsburg Plaza and the gardens of the Arboretum.

Palmer Fern Dell

The Palmer Fern Dell was designed by landscape architect Naud Burnett and dedicated to Eugenia Leftwich Palmer. It opened in 1990 and was expanded in 2003. The garden is one acre in size and features over three hundred species of ferns. The Fern Dell is a microclimate of acidic, well-drained, soilless media. The bark and the peat beds make it possible to grow many plants that would otherwise not flourish in Dallas due to the alkalinity, or high pH, of the water and soil in North Texas. Mountain laurels (kalmia), pieris (andromeda), camellias, and azaleas flourish in this environment.

The fog system, an MEE II Cloudmaker, was developed for NASA to study cloud formations and their effect on flight. On hot, dry days, the fog system can drop the temperature in the dell by twenty degrees.

The granite Kasuga Lantern, which was created in Kyoto in the nineteenth century is located on the western side of the stream. It was presented to the Dallas Arboretum by the Japan-America Society on May 19, 1995. It is similar in design to lanterns that line the pathways at the Kasuga Shrine in Nara.

Jonsson Color Garden

The Jonsson Color Garden, designed by Dallas landscape architect Naud Burnett, was named for Margaret Elizabeth Jonsson and given by her husband Erik Jonsson, who founded Texas Instruments and formerly served as mayor of Dallas. The garden was opened in March 1990 and is six and a half acres. There are three Jonsson Color Garden Areas: the Upper and Middle Gardens, closest to the DeGolyer House and planted with seasonal color four times a year, and the Lower Gardens featuring seasonal perennial plants. During March and April, this garden bursts into bloom with daffodils, azaleas, tulips, flowering peach trees, and dogwood during the Dallas Blooms Festival. Fall and winter seasons feature chrysanthemums, pansies, and a plethora of cool-weather flowers.

Many shade trees in the Jonsson Color Garden are original to the DeGolyer estate and were incorporated into the overall design, which now includes additional plantings of flowering peach trees, crape myrtles, and dogwoods along with various oak trees.

The ironwork handrail leading down from the house into the Jonsson Color Garden was produced by Joe Nesterole, who did the ironwork for the DeGolyer House in the 1930s. The smooth stone columns at the DeGolyer pergola are of native Lueders Limestone, and the rough columns and walls are of Texas limestone quarried near Granbury, Texas. Their design was copied from the original columns at the back of the DeGolyer House. The smaller walkways are bordered with Pennsylvania blue-green slate, and the broader ones are exposed aggregate paths that consist of green serpentine marble from Marble Falls, Texas.

The sculpture Grande Amanti is on loan from the Dallas Museum of Art.

Of particular note is the impressive collection of azaleas representing two hundred fifty cultivars, including Huang azaleas.

21

DeGolyer House

Designed by architects Denman Scott and Burton Schutt, the DeGolyer House reflects the Spanish Colonial Revival style, and is listed on the National Register of Historic Places. It was originally called "Rancho Encinal" because of the many live oak trees on the property. The house is twenty-one thousand square feet and contains thirteen rooms, seven baths, and seven chimneys—each featuring a different design to match the accompanying fireplace. Nell and Everette DeGolyer insisted that the house be designed to look one hundred years old when finished, and the plan takes full advantage of the lake and garden views. It was undoubtedly laid out to accommodate existing trees and plants that were part of the original forty-four-acre dairy farm.

The photographs included are of the original house. As the DeGolyer interior is in the process of a decor restoration at this time, any photographs taken would not be representative of it today.

Dann Talley Kincheloe Courtyard

The back of the DeGolyer House was considered to be the front door, with the beauty of White Rock Lake before it. Susan Kincheloe Holman and her family reinvigorated this area, providing extended brick walkways and plantings surrounding the house. It is named for Dann Talley Kincheloe, Susan's mother, who was a community leader and active in many organizations, including her garden club.

Nancy's Garden

Nancy's Garden was originally Mrs. Nell DeGolyer's personal garden. Renovated in 1986 and dedicated to the children of Nancy Dillard Lyons, it now includes child-sized benches as well as the sculpture *Thank Heaven for Little Girls* by Gary Price. The Bill Dillard Family has renovated the plantings and lighting of this treasured area of the arboretum. The garden is embraced by soft pink crape myrtles and azaleas, and it is filled seasonally with pastel annual color.

A Woman's Garden

A Woman's Garden was completed in the fall of 1997. A gift from the Women's Council of the Dallas Arboretum, together with bond funds from the City of Dallas, the specifically designed acreage on the White Rock Lake side of the DeGolyer home is dedicated to the spirit and essence of women and was designed by landscape architect Morgan Wheelock, whose other projects include the International Peace Garden and the U.S. Armed Forces Memorial Garden in Cannes.

The first section represents the strength of a woman with characteristics that are controlled, orderly, formal, strong, forceful, structured, organized, powerful, and reflective. The many garden rooms lining the main terrace offer areas for reflection. Features include the Sunset Oak Garden with a seventy-five-year old live oak tree, the Sloping Rose Garden, the Harmony Repose with its Infinity II Windharp, and the Fragrant Longue Vue Garden.

The middle level features the Grand Entrance, dedicated to Carrie Marcus Neiman by Neiman Marcus on its 90th Anniversary; the Stepped Fountain, shining through its shimmering tiles and its pools flowing one onto the next, showing generations of women helping other generations of women; and the Main Terrace Garden, given by

Dee and Charles Wyly, which leads to the Reflective Basin, a large rectangular pool, given by Mary Silverthorne.

The lower level includes the Pecan Parterre Garden, the Poetry Garden, the Lower Rose Garden, the Flowering Vitex Walk, and the Lower Waterview Garden.

The second part of A Woman's Garden is concave, enclosing and turning in on itself, representing the characteristics of a woman that are nurturing, relaxed, spontaneous, mothering, self-sacrificing, mysterious, and magical. One area features flowing creeks, narrow winding paths, and water features, suggesting the beginning of life—the Genesis Garden.

It also contains one of the state's largest and most comprehensive collections of specimen Japanese maples. The Stone Bridge, given by Jan and Fred Hegi, is dedicated to Warren Hill Johnson, the landscape architect who interpreted the design of A Woman's Garden. It traverses the stream which emanates from the Fernwood Fold. Above the site, the Pulpit Garden, a heartshaped stone structure, overlooks the Meadow and affords a view of the entire garden.

McCasland Sunken Garden

The McCasland Sunken Garden was designed by Warren Hill Johnson and was a gift from Phyllis and Tom McCasland. The site is a reinterpretation of the original Sunken Garden and features tree forms called rose of sharon, flowering perennials, and a colonnade of sculpted plants, English jardinieres, as well as seasonal plantings. The sculpture *Chico y Chica* by Victor Salmones rests at the top of a beautifully cascading water feature and was given by the Meadows Foundation.

Boswell Family Garden

The Boswell Family Garden was designed by Warren Hill Johnson, landscape architect of Fallcreek Garden. Named El Inesperaldo, meaning "the unexpected," the garden was a gift from Dr. George Boswell to his wife Veta and their three daughters, Kama Koudelka, Brianna Brown, and Maia Boswell-Penc. Opened in March 2006, the garden features a backdrop of Earth-Kind and antique roses, symmetrical and serpentine plantings mirrored by topiary hollies, and cubed hedges accented by red and yellow-leafed barberry hedges in a double-helical configuration.

Lyda Bunker Hunt Paseo de Flores

The Lyda Bunker Hunt Paseo de Flores was designed by landscape architect Luis Sergio Santana of the Slaney Santana Group in Dallas, Texas. This garden is dedicated to Lyda Bunker Hunt, wife of H.L. Hunt, and was funded in 1985 with City of Dallas bonds and donations from the Hunt Family and Dallas Arboretum and Botanical Society volunteers. The Paseo de Flores, Spanish for "walkway of flowers" was opened in March 1991.

The Paseo is a quarter-mile long with varying widths; it contains twenty-five thousand square feet of bedded plant area and connects the main public entry on the south end of the arboretum with the Camp House and Lay Ornamental Garden on the north end. Many of the oldest trees in the arboretum line the Paseo.

The yaupon holly topiary, located on the northeast corner of the crossing of the Paseo and DeGolyer drive, is perfectly suited to the climate and conditions of Dallas. It was a gift to the arboretum from Rob Collins, who planted it in his yard in 1968 and began to shape it into its present form in 1984, utilizing the art of shaping woody plants called topiary. The tree was moved at a cost of three thousand dollars, which is not surprising considering its root ball is eight feet in diameter.

The beautiful ornamental urns along this walkway and at the entry of A Woman's Garden were rescued from the Woolf Brothers building, formerly known as the Dreyfuss building, in downtown Dallas before it was demolished in 1982. They were a gift to the Arboretum from the Historic Preservation League of Dallas. These urns serve as gateways and framing vistas, marking the entrances to the gardens.

Martha Brooks Camellia Garden

The Martha Brooks Camellia Garden was designed by Warren Hill Johnson and is dedicated to Martha Brooks, wife of Dick Brooks, retired CEO of Central and South West Corporation. Funded by the employees of Central and South West Corporation, the garden was opened to the public in January 2000. The plantings feature two hundred camellias and over thirty different cultivars. Blooming generally occurs in this garden in the cold winter months.

Toad Corners

One of the most popular areas at the Dallas Arboretum for the viewing by adults and especially the joy obtained by children is Toad Corners. Located at the end of the Crape Myrtle Allee, children can see the beginning of the life of a toad in tadpole sculptures at the entrance to the walkway. At the end of their walk, they discover four bronze toads five feet tall spewing twenty feet of water at the same time onto a round sphere in the center of the court. It is an unusual day when you do not see children enjoying the spray of water in this area or hear the laughing and giggling that this brings to the garden. The area is enclosed by a hedge of American Hornbeam trees, a deciduous type native to East Texas. This part of the renovation of the Arboretum was done by the Communities Foundation of Texas in 1994. Toad Corners, produced by the Johnson Atelier Foundry, is but one of several reasons why the Dallas Arboretum is a favorite family destination in our city.

Crape Myrtle Allee

Crape Myrtle Allee was conceptualized by SAW Group, a Dallas landscape and architectural firm. It was funded originally by the Communities Foundation and opened to the public in 1994. The Allee features a replaced lane of crape myrtle trees originally planted by the DeGolyers. Marking the entrance to the Allee are the water features entitled Polliwogs, showing a tadpole that will later become a toad. Paved with Pennsylvania Bluestone, the Allee runs from the Paseo to Toad Corners. Crape Myrtle Allee has been permanently endowed by Peggy Braecklein.

Trial Gardens

The Trial Gardens offer visibility for plant selections on the market and those soon to be available. Visitors can observe how plants perform under the extreme conditions of Dallas.

One part of the mission of the Dallas Arboretum and Botanical Society (DABS) is to research and develop new plant selections for use in displays at the Arboretum, while providing helpful information for institutions, commercial plant producers, and home gardeners. The research done here helps identify plant varieties that will flourish under low maintenance conditions.

The Dallas Arboretum was designated an All-America Selections Trial Garden in 2002 and opened the exhibit to the public in March 2003. The Dallas Arboretum is the thirty-first trial site.

The Dallas Arboretum Trial Gardens have become the premiere site for testing the ability of new plant materials to withstand climatic extremes. Over three thousand plants are submitted each year for evaluation by over three hundred fifty gardening companies worldwide.

Camp House

The Camp House property, purchased by Alex and Roberta Camp, covers twenty-two acres at the north end of the Dallas Arboretum. It was designed by acclaimed architect John Staub in the Latin Colonial style, with wonderful Art Deco interiors. Each room off the entry has three exposures to the outdoors. The western exposure presents spectacular views of White Rock Lake, especially from its patios and terraces. The entrance to the Camp House features the Fogelson Fountain, underwritten by the late Greer Garson in memory of her husband, the late Colonel Buddy Fogelson. There are connections between the Camp family and the DeGolyer family in addition to the geographic proximity of their houses. Everett DeGolyer Jr.'s first wife was Roberta Camp's cousin, and his second wife was Alex Camp's stepniece. Nell DeGolyer's nephew-in-law, Ralph Rogers, was instrumental in buying the Camp House with other friends of the botanic gardens and holding it until the Arboretum's later purchase and ownership transfer to the City of Dallas. The Eugene McDermott Foundation and private donors have helped with the renovation, engaging Emily Summers and Associates for interior design.

Martin Rutchik Concert Lawn and Stage

The lakeside lawn of the Alex Camp House and the stage at its base are named the Martin Rutchick Concert Lawn in honor of Dallas businessman, Martin Rutchik. Funds for its development were provided by his wife, Nancy. The trees and the lighting near the concert stage and the walkway to it were also given by Mrs. Rutchik.

Instead of a permanent stage, the base is just eighteen inches above the ground. Instead of a backdrop, the stage has a semicircle of magnolias, Chinese fringe flowers, and holly.

Tickets to the family friendly concert series in the spring, summer, and fall sell out quickly each season. The lawn is filled with concert-goers on some evenings; other times, it is the site for some of our city's most beautiful weddings. The lighting in the front and back of the Camp House was provided by the family and friends of George Jalonick.

Lay Ornamental Garden

Anchoring the north end of the arboretum is the Lay Ornamental Garden, which showcases hundreds of perennial plants adapted to the North Texas area. Based on principles laid down by horticultural designer Gertrude Jekyll of England, the garden features shaded areas of flower collections, lilies, irises, verbena, a delightful rose garden, as well as a collection of hardy palms. A magnificent pergola crowns this beautiful area with an unusual falling water curtain, a multilevel pond for fish and aquatic plants, and an overhead lattice covered with blue wisteria and orange trumpet vine. Scattered through the gardens is a collection of bronze wildlife sculptures commissioned and donated by Dallas businessman and philanthropist Trammell Crow. This garden was a gift from Mimi Lay Hodges and was given in the name of her husband, Herman Lay.

Festivals and Horticultural Displays

Dallas Blooms is a six-week-long festival and is the largest outdoor floral festival in the south. The centerpiece of this event is the display of four hundred and fifty thousand spring-blooming bulbs—including tulips, daffodils, Dutch iris, and hyacinth, in addition to two hundred and fifty thousand pansies, violas, and poppies. The most beautiful days of the Dallas Blooms Festival are during the mass flowering of our collection of three thousand azaleas amidst the bulb display. The theme of each festival is usually interpreted in topiary form by the gardens'

horticultural staff. Family-friendly activities include wagon rides, games for children, and musical events.

Autumn at the Arboretum allows visitors to discover the rich colors of over one hundred and fifty thousand flowers and invites guests to stroll through the pumpkin patch, see a house made out of pumpkins, play in a hay bale maze, and listen to live music. The Arboretum also celebrates May Flowers by showcasing over eighty thousand spring-blooming annuals in full color.

The Arboretum in Every Season

The Dallas Arboretum has a natural charm throughout the year, whether you choose to come for a winter walk or stroll in the cool breezes of autumn; whether you enjoy us best during the changing colors of spring or if your favorite time is when we showcase the powerful summer color offered by tropicals and summer annuals. If you have come once, we know you will want to visit again.

The Arboretum is also a place that is welcoming to all ages, all nationalities, and all interests. There are few days that you do not see a bride being photographed in the garden, sweethearts walking hand-in-hand, or a multigenerational family visiting the garden together, for there is something for all of them to enjoy. We also have nature lovers, gardeners with keen interests in the latest cultivars, photographers at seemingly every turn, and many languages spoken gently throughout the garden. And sometimes we have people who just want to escape their routine and revel in the beauty that nature can provide. Their special joy is a place on a bench under a graceful tree overlooking our grounds whose beauty often defies description.

Lastly, this garden is a place of joy, comfort, and relaxation. You rarely hear children crying, but you surely hear them giggling with happiness. At the end of each day, some things are heard again and again as guests exit, "We should come here more often" and "This was a good day."

So as we share these final pictures of our garden during various times of the year, we hope that they and the other selections made in this compendium will make you want to plan your next trip to the Dallas Arboretum. We will warmly welcome you and *Let Nature Nurture You.*